VAMPIRES

MARC TYLER NOBLEMAN

D1330433

www.raintreepublishers.co.uk
Visit our website to find out more inform

To order:
☎ Phone 44 (0) 1865 888112
▤ Send a fax to 44 (0) 1865 314091
💻 Visit the Raintree bookshop at **www.ra**
  our catalogue and order online.

BARNET LIBRARIES	
11-Dec-06	PETERS
CNF	

First published in Great Britain by
Raintree, Halley Court, Jordan Hill,
Oxford OX2 8EJ, part of Harcourt
Education. Raintree is a registered
trademark of Harcourt Education Ltd.

© Harcourt Education Ltd 2007
First published in paperback in 2007.
The moral right of the proprietor has been asserted.

All rights reserved. No part of this publication
may be reproduced, stored in a retrieval system, or
transmitted in any form or by any means, electronic,
mechanical, photocopying, recording, or otherwise,
without either the prior written permission of the
publishers or a licence permitting restricted copying in
the United Kingdom issued by the Copyright Licensing
Agency Ltd, 90 Tottenham Court Road, London W1T
4LP (www.cla.co.uk).

Editorial: Louise Galpine, Rosie Gordon, Dave Harris,
and Stig Vatland
Design: Victoria Bevan and Bigtop
Picture Research: Mica Brancic and Elaine Willis
Production: Camilla Crask

Originated by Chroma Graphics Pte. Ltd
Printed and bound in China by WKT

10 digit ISBN 1 406 20348 3 (hardback)
13 digit IBSN 978 1 406 20348 6
11 10 09 08 07
10 9 8 7 6 5 4 3 2 1

10 digit ISBN 1 406 20369 6 (paperback)
13 digit IBSN 978 1 406 20369 1
12 11 10 09 08
10 9 8 7 6 5 4 3 2 1

British Library Cataloguing in Publication Data

Nobleman, Marc Tyler
  Vampires. – (Atomic)
  1.Vampires – Juvenile literature
  I.Title
  398.2'1
A full catalogue record for this book is available
from the British Library.

Acknowledgements

The publishers would like to thank the following for
permission to reproduce photographs: AKG p. **21**;
Alamy/The Marsden Archive p. **17**; Corbis/Bettmann
pp. **5**, **6 right**, **14**, **26**; Getty Images/Nacivet p. **29**;
Getty Images/John Kobal Foundation p. **9**; Getty
Images/Time Life Pictures p. **25** (J. R. Eyerman); Jerry
Wolf/The Kobal Collection/20th Century Fox Television
p. **27**; Rex Features/Everett Collection p. **13**; The Kobal
Collection/Columbia Tri–Star/Zoetrope p. **6 left**; The
Kobal Collection/Dirk Prods/Getty p. **10**; TopFoto/
Sibbick/Fortean p. **22**; www.chartaonline p. **15**. Cover
photograph reproduced with permission of Corbis.

The publishers would like to thank Diana Bentley,
Nancy Harris, and Dee Reid for their assistance in the
preparation of this book.

Every effort has been made to contact copyright
holders of any material reproduced in this book. Any
omissions will be rectified in subsequent printings if
notice is given to the publishers.

Disclaimer

All the Internet addresses (URLs) given in this book
were valid at the time of going to press. However,
due to the dynamic nature of the Internet, some
addresses may have changed, or sites may have
changed or ceased to exist since publication. While
the author and publishers regret any inconvenience
this may cause readers, no responsibility for any such
changes can be accepted by either the author or the
publishers.

Contents

Some words are printed in bold, **like this**. You can find out what they mean in the glossary. You can also look in the box at the bottom of the page where the word first appears.

Do Vampires Exist?

Many cultures have legends about vampires. Some people believe that these legends are true. Others do not.

What are vampires?

A vampire is said to be a creature that drinks human blood. Vampires do this to survive. Often they need no other food or drink.

Vampires are **undead**. They are humans who died and have come back to life. People bitten by vampires might become vampires themselves.

Vampires sleep in their graves or coffins during the day. They rise at night in search of blood.

Many countries around the world have their own vampire legends.

ENGLAND
HUNGARY
ROMANIA
BULGARIA
JAPAN
USA
PUERTO RICO
MEXICO
JAMAICA
BRAZIL
MALAWI
CHILE
ARGENTINA
AUSTRALIA

Vampires are frightening to many people, but vampires are afraid of things, too.

| legend | story from the past that is not always true |
| undead | describes a creature that has died and then come back to life |

The way vampires look has changed over the years, but their thirst for blood has stayed the same.

WHAT VAMPIRES LOOK LIKE

In the past people believed that vampires looked like monsters. Many had **fangs**; in addition some had long fingernails that were like claws.

Vampire features

Vampires had different features in different countries. In Bulgaria, vampires had only one nostril. In Mexico, they had no skin on their skulls.

Vampires started to look more human in the 1900s. Today, the common image of a vampire is a man dressed in fine clothes and a long black cape.

Deadly fact!

Today, people say that vampires can look like any one of us. They want to blend in.

fang   sharp tooth

VAMPIRE POWERS

In some **legends** vampires can do things that people cannot. They can live forever if they have enough blood to drink. Some vampires are very strong.

Animal nature

Some stories say that vampires can change into bats, foxes, or other animals. They can also change into mist. Some vampires can control animals, such as wolves or rats.

Other stories reveal that vampires can fly, even when they are not in the form of a bat. Some vampires can climb walls like a lizard.

Deadly fact!

Legends say that vampires have no reflection in mirrors and cannot be photographed.

It is said that vampires have no shadow.

Some people used to wear a necklace made of garlic. They thought this would protect them from vampires.

VAMPIRE WEAKNESSES

Vampires have unusual powers. But they also have unusual weaknesses.

* Splashing **holy water** on vampires can burn them. Other religious items scare them away.
* Vampires cannot be near garlic.
* Vampires are unable to cross running water, such as streams.
* Vampires cannot enter a home unless they are invited.

What do you think?

Why do you think vampires are scared of so many things?

| holy water | water that a religious leader has blessed |

How to Kill a Vampire

Since vampires are already dead, there are special ways to kill them again.

* You can kill vampires by touching them with a **sacred** object, such as a cross.
* Touching them with garlic also kills them.
* Vampires die if they are burned or if their heads are cut off.
* Sunlight can destroy vampires.
* In some stories, knives and bullets can kill vampires.

Deadly fact!

Some cultures believed that stuffing a vampire's left sock with stones and tossing it into a river would kill the vampire. He would jump in after the sock and drown.

Legends say that vampires die if a wooden stake is pushed through their heart.

sacred — holy
stake — pointed piece of wood

Even well-dressed vampires, such as Dracula, sleep in cold, hard coffins.

INTRODUCING DRACULA

In 1897, the world met a new kind of vampire. That year, the novel *Dracula* by Bram Stoker was published.

A gentleman vampire

The main character in the book is Count Dracula. He is a vampire who lives in Europe. His castle is in the mountains of Transylvania.

Dracula is different from the vampires that came before him. He is smart, polite, wealthy, and well-dressed. However, he is dangerous. Like all vampires, he has a thirst for blood.

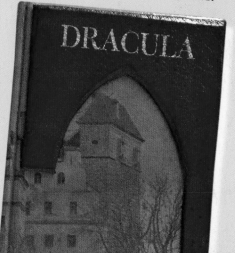

Bram Stoker's novel was a best-seller.

DRACULA

Deadly fact!

Dracula has appeared in books, films, TV programmes, comic books, and video games.

VLAD TEPES

Dracula is a fictional character. However, Bram Stoker may have named Dracula after a real person, Vlad Tepes.

Son of the devil

In the mid-1500s, Vlad Tepes was the ruler of Wallachia. Today, Wallachia is part of Romania. Vlad was also called Vlad III the Impaler and Vlad Dracula.

Vlad was not a vampire, but he was evil. During his **reign**, thousands of people were killed in painful ways. His favourite method was to **impale** them on wooden **stakes**.

What do you think?

Do you think Dracula was based on Vlad Tepes?

fictional	describes a story that has been made up
impale	put a sharp wooden stick through someone's body
reign	period during which a royal leader is in power

Vlad killed many people in very cruel ways.

What do you think?

Why do you think Dracula might be based on Elizabeth Báthory?

Báthory thought that bathing in girls' blood would keep her young and beautiful.

THE BLOOD COUNTESS

Another person Dracula may be based on is Elizabeth Báthory. Like Vlad, she was not a vampire. But she was accused of killing many people for their blood.

Horrible crimes

Báthory was a **countess** who lived in Hungary. In the late 1500s, she murdered hundreds of girls in her castle. Four of her servants helped her. It is believed that Báthory took baths in the murdered girls' blood. Some people say that she also drank the blood of the prettiest girls.

In 1610, Báthory was imprisoned in her own castle. She died four years later.

countess   noblewoman, member of the upper class

VAMPIRES AROUND THE WORLD

Many vampire stories come from Eastern Europe. But other places have vampire **legends**, too.

* In Australia, people are scared of the yara-ma-yha-who. This creature has long, **tentacle**-like fingers. It uses suckers on its fingers to drink blood.

* People in Jamaica tell tales of the ol' higue. During the day, *ol' higue* looks like an old woman. At night, it becomes a flying ball of fire and looks for blood.

* The Japanese kappa is said to live in rivers. If a person offers a kappa some cucumber, it may be kind. If not, the kappa will drink the person's blood.

| tentacle | long, arm-like body part |

What do you think?

Why do you think so many countries have vampire legends?

This picture shows a scene from a Chinese vampire film.

The *chupacabra* feeds on small animals.

Vampires Today

Stories about vampires are still occasionally in the news.

Short, hairy, and scary

Throughout the 1990s, people in Puerto Rico and Mexico found dead farm animals. It seemed like something had sucked out their blood. Some people think that the killer was the *chupacabra*. **Legends** describe the *chupacabra* as a short, hairy creature with spikes down its back.

- In 2002, people in the African country of Malawi claimed they were attacked by vampires.
- In 2005, some people in Birmingham said a man on the street had bitten them.

Nobody has explained what really caused these events.

Deadly fact!

El chupacabra means "the goat sucker" in Spanish.

VAMPIRE BATS

Vampire bats drink the blood of animals, such as horses. They do not kill the animals they bite. Once in a while, they try to drink human blood, but they are usually scared of humans.

Vampire bat homes

Vampire bats are found in Argentina, Brazil, Chile, and other countries in South America. They also live in Mexico and the southern United States. Vampire bats live in dark areas, such as caves.

Could these be the real vampires?

Deadly fact!

Vampire bats were named after vampires, not the other way around.

Vampire bats do not suck blood. They lap it up, like a dog slurping up water from a bowl.

Nosferatu is still scary today.

premiered   shown for the first time

VAMPIRES ON SCREEN

Vampires may be scary, but they can also be entertaining.

Vampires in films

In 1922, the silent film *Nosferatu* was released. Then, in 1931, *Dracula* **premiered**. These films showed different types of vampire, but both were creepy. People still watch them today. Many other vampire films have been made since.

In entertainment, some vampires are good. A vampire called The Count is a character on the TV programme *Sesame Street*. In comic books, a vampire called Blade is a superhero.

Buffy the Vampire Slayer was a popular TV show that began in 1997.

ARE VAMPIRES REAL?

In the past many people believed in vampires. Today, fewer people do.

Modern vampires?

Sometimes when people are sick, they need blood to help them get better. Also, if someone has a bad accident, they may lose a lot of blood. In these cases, a doctor gives them blood with an **injection**. These people are not vampires. The doctor gets the blood from men and women who want to help sick people.

Scientists have not proved that vampires exist. If **undead** vampires with strange powers are out there, they are very good at hiding. These days, not many people believe in scary monsters such as vampires. However, many people still find them interesting.

What do you think?

Why do you think people are still interested in vampires?

injection   when a needle is used to put a substance into the body

There will always be people who think vampires are real.

Glossary

countess noblewoman, member of the upper class

fang sharp tooth

fictional describes a story that has been made up

holy water water that a religious leader has blessed

impale put a sharp wooden stick through someone's body

injection when a needle is used to put a substance into the body

legend story from the past that is not always true

premiered shown for the first time

reign period during which a royal leader is in power

sacred holy

stake pointed piece of wood

tentacle long, arm-like body part

undead describes a creature that has died and then come back to life

Want to know more?

Books

✴ *Real Vampires*, Daniel Cohen (Cobblehill, 1995)

✴ *Vampires*, Angela Cybulski, ed. (Greenhaven, 2003)

✴ *Vampire Bats (The Library of Bats)*, Emily Raabe (PowerKids, 2003)

Websites

✴ www.factmonster.com/spot/ dracula9.html
This website tells you all about vampires, especially Dracula.

✴ www.pantheon.org/articles/v/ vampire.html
Here you can find a lot of information about vampires.

If you liked this Atomic book, why don't you try these...?

Index

Notes for adults
Use the following questions to guide children towards identifying features of discussion text:
Can you give examples of different opinions on page 4?
Can you find examples of present tense language on page 8?
Can you give an example of a statement of the issue on page 11?
Can you find examples of connectives on page 27?
Can you give an example of recommendation on page 28?